W.C.P.C.

'Joe Orton has had many imitators but the great virtue of Nigel Williams' *W.C.P.C.* is that it matches both the candour and the daring of its dramatic predecessor's best work. It is a spiralling comic nightmare in which a raw, reactionary young P.C. from Basingstoke joins the Indecency Unit of the Met's Vice Squad and embarks on a round-the-toilets clean-up campaign only to observe that everyone around him (both in and out of uniform) is as bent as nine-bob notes.' Steven Grant *Time Out*

'lavatorially festive' Michael Billington *Guardian*

'brilliant black comedy which gives an altogether new meaning to Queen's Evidence' Sheridan Morley, *Punch*

'a manic farce in the Alice in Wonderland tradition. The Alice in question is a bright young recruit who strays into the Vice Squad determined to do his duty for Queen and country only to find the entire department manned (and manhandled) by more queens than even Henry VIII could handle.' Jack Tinker, *Daily Mail*

W.C.P.C. was first staged at the Half Moon Theatre, London, in April 1982.

W.C.P.C.

NIGEL WILLIAMS

A Methuen New Theatrescript
Methuen · London

A METHUEN PAPERBACK

First published as a paperback original in 1983 by Methuen London Ltd,
11 New Fetter Lane, London EC4P 4EE
Copyright © 1983 by Nigel Williams
Printed by Expression Printers Ltd, London N7

ISBN 0 413 51920 1

CAUTION
All rights whatsoever in this play are strictly reserved and application for performance etc.
should be made before rehearsals begin to Judy Daish Associates, 122 Wigmore Street,
London W1H 9FE. No performance may be given unless a licence has been obtained.

For Pam and Barry

W.C.P.C. was first presented at the Half Moon Theatre, London, on 29 April 1982, with the following cast:

CHIEF SUPERINTENDENT FEAVER	Leonard Fenton
P.C. SIMON	Phil Smeeton
SERGEANT HARRIS	Bill Stewart
P.C. JAMIESON	Derek Thompson
MAN	James Winston
COMMANDER WESTWICH	Robert Stephens
DORIS	James Winston
SHAW	Alan Ford
CLEM BREEN	William Hoyland

Directed by Pam Brighton
Decor by David Fielding
Lighting by Andy Phillips
Musical Director Rick Lloyd
Choreographer Pauline Lewis
Assistant Director Will Harde

ACT ONE

Sousa March music.

Scene One

An interview room. FEAVER *and*
SIMON. SIMON *is a young police constable
fresh out of training school and* CHIEF
SUPERINTENDENT FEAVER *is a senior
man with many years of experience behind
him.*

FEAVER: Don't be nervous. You are . . .

SIMON: Simon, sir.

FEAVER: I am Chief Superintendent
Feaver. Working at the moment in
personnel allocations. But based
elsewhere. Now . . . Your reports
from . . .

SIMON: Basingstoke, sir.

FEAVER: Basingstoke, are excellent.
You've done very well.

SIMON: Thank you sir.

FEAVER: Now – you've had two years beat
work and now you're back at college on
the understanding we'd be looking at you
for a special unit – right?

SIMON: That's right, sir.

FEAVER: You're a young lad. Your first
posting is going to be quite crucial. I see
your parents keep a shop.

SIMON: That's right, sir. In Basingstoke,
sir.

FEAVER: Now, what sort of crime attracts
you?

SIMON: Sorry sir?

FEAVER: Are you interested in
immigrants at all?

SIMON: How do you mean, sir?

FEAVER: People from overseas, Pakistan,
India, the Caribbean living here
illegally . . .

SIMON: Not really sir. There aren't many
of them in Basingstoke. Well, there may
be but I haven't actually run across any of
them if you see what I mean, sir.

FEAVER: No.

SIMON: It's probably a bit far for them I
suppose.

FEAVER: Yes.

SIMON: I imagine you find them near
airports and so on.

FEAVER: You do yes . . . How about vice?

SIMON: Er . . .

FEAVER: Much vice in Basingstoke?

SIMON: Not much sir, since they built the
M3 mind . . .

FEAVER: Vice is of course, incredibly
popular. Everyone wants to get into vice.
I'm up to here with applications for
people to get into vice . . .

SIMON: For a bit, sir. Till I get settled.
Anyway I'm . . .

FEAVER: Bound up in the job. I know.
Occupational hazard of our job (police
work) lad. Drink with your mates in the
force, play soccer with them, get cut off
from the outside world.

SIMON: I know, sir.

FEAVER: Lose touch with reality.
Anyway, this won't get the dog washed.
Where are we going to send you, that's
the question. I'm going back to my unit in
a week or two.

SIMON: Aren't you from Personnel, sir?

FEAVER: Gracious heaven, no. I'm Chief
Superintendent in a working unit – had a
barney with the powers that be, got
myself sent off to Personnel for a spell.

SIMON: Where do you work, sir?

FEAVER: Me? I'm in the ISQ, the 'I ask
you', we call it.

SIMON: What does your section do, sir?

FEAVER: It's a bit hush hush. Not many
people know about us. The outside world
never hears about us if we can help it.

SIMON: What sort of area, sir?

FEAVER: Oh, all over.

SIMON: No, I meant what sort of . . .

FEAVER: It's related to vice.

SIMON: It must be very serious, sir.

FEAVER: You're keen lad aren't you? All
right Simon, I'll go out on a limb for you.
You seem a decent lad and I'll go out on a
limb for you. I'll send you to ISQ. Only
don't tell them I sent you.

SIMON: Why not, sir?

FEAVER: You know how the police force is, by now Simon, at my level. Departmental jealousy.

SIMON: Right, sir.

FEAVER: Simon you'll have to swear on your mother's grave to keep mum. Once you're in the ISQ that's it. The only way out is to get yourself discharged.

SIMON: I can't wait, sir.

FEAVER: Me neither.

Reprise Sousa March.

Scene Two

The classroom.

HARRIS: Where's the new lad?

JAMIESON: Simon, sir?

HARRIS: How many times have I told you to address your fellow constables by their surnames?

JAMIESON: Plenty of times, sir, but that is his surname.

HARRIS: Uh. Well, he's late.

JAMIESON: I saw him down in physical training, Sarge.

HARRIS: All the same these new lads. Still he comes with glowing reports.

JAMIESON: He's dead keen, Sarge.

HARRIS: We'll get started anyway.

Enter SIMON:

SIMON: Sorry I'm late Sergeant.

HARRIS: Playing too hard son?

SIMON: Right sir, sorry sir.

SIMON *sits.*

HARRIS: For the beginning I should watch and learn. O.K.? P.C. Simon. Watch and learn. In case you didn't know today we are doing Toilet Procedure Part Two which, for your information, carries on from Toilet Procedures Part One. Wouldn't you say so, Jamieson?

JAMIESON: Right, Sarge.

HARRIS: Well, any questions Jameison? Anything to sort out or do we know it all? Perhaps we know it all.

SIMON *raises his hand.*

Simon?

SIMON: I was going to ask Sarge, how we might expect the suspect to behave in the toilet?

HARRIS: Good question, Simon and that brings us right into Toilet Procedure Part Two. The answer to that is – at first the suspect may, well, appear like any normal user of the toilet.

SIMON: Very much like you or I, Sergeant?

HARRIS: Very much, Simon. But after a while you'll notice one very significant thing . . . Anyone any ideas as to what it might be?

JAMIESON: Effeminate gestures, sir?

HARRIS: Good try, Jamieson, not quite . . .

SIMON: Movement of the hips, sir?

HARRIS: No, no. We're in a toilet not a night club. There's our suspect. He's in the lavatory. I approach him so . . .

SIMON: Writing on the walls, Sarge?

HARRIS: Hardly, hardly. No. The first thing we notice is that he is spending a hell of a lot more time in there than is normal. So we'll put that on the board as 'T' for time.

JAMIESON: Sarge –

HARRIS: Yes, Jamieson?

JAMIESON: After exactly how long should we consider a suspect a suspect?

HARRIS: Good question. We reckon it takes from fifty seconds to two minutes twenty in the urinals and up to ten minutes in a closed cubicle.

SIMON: Sarge?

HARRIS: Yes . . .

SIMON: Can one be flexible about that?

HARRIS: I think that any longer than that and you couldn't be called flexible, Simon.

SIMON: It's just that –

HARRIS: Yes lad, what's your problem.

SIMON: I mean Sarge, obviously one's worried about making a wrong arrest and that if someone has taken a long time it may not necessarily mean that he is a suspect.

HARRIS: Good point, Simon. Good point. So what do you think we do after we've established the 'T' for time test? Our suspect has been in the place for three minutes in the open area or for a quarter of an hour in the closed cubicle – What do we do?

JAMIESON: Hide, Sarge.

HARRIS: Come on lad, we've hidden already.

JAMIESON: Keep our eyes pealed, Sarge?

HARRIS: Ye – es. But . . . what else . . .

JAMIESON: Approach him, Sarge.

HARRIS: Very good, approach him . . . and?

SIMON: Warn him, Sarge.

HARRIS: *Warn* him Simon, what on earth do you mean, warn him?

SIMON: Warn him that he is taking too long over his business, Sarge.

HARRIS: Simon, you are a police officer, not a nanny. Think. Come on, think.

JAMIESON: Er . . .

HARRIS: Yes?

JAMIESON: Entice him, Sarge.

HARRIS: *Correct.* And how do we do that, Jamieson?

JAMIESON: By gesture, by voice and by expression.

HARRIS: Oh you would, would you P.C. Jamieson. What gesture may I ask, what voice and what expression? Mmm?

JAMIESON: Well, Sarge, I would give him to understand that I was homosexual.

HARRIS: Would you indeed, Jamieson.

JAMIESON: Yes, sir, I would.

HARRIS: And just how would you do that?

JAMIESON: I might say . . . 'I'm a homosexual'.

HARRIS: ye – es . . . and . . . ?

JAMIESON: Er . . . 'Hullo'.

HARRIS: Well, you're making a pig's arse out of this and no mistake. I'll tell you, you must *not* entice him by gesture, by voice or by expression – you remembered the beginning Jamieson, but you forgot that important little word. Now how does it go on? You must not entice him by gesture, by voice or by expression but you must allow him to think . . .

JAMIESON: Allow him to think . . .

HARRIS: Allow him to think . . .

JAMIESON: Allow him to think you might not be averse to intimacy without directly suggesting it.

HARRIS: Good . . . You must behave like an ordinary member of the public who, although normal could be mistaken for a homosexual. O.K.? Now when he approaches you – wait for him to make the advances and then, what next, Simon?

SIMON: Reciprocate, sir.

HARRIS: Simon, are you out of your mind?

SIMON: I thought, sir, in order to get more evidence . . .

JAMIESON: Arrest him, Sarge.

HARRIS: Thank you, Jamieson. I worry about you, lad, I really do. Anyway let me move on to your first assignment, which is the public convenience off the junction of Vauxhall Bridge Road and Cremlin Gardens. And for this duty you will need operational kit which consists of . . . Yer pansy boys are very fond of rings, so here they are. Rings, silver, third finger of the left hand for the use of. Cravat, silk, observed to be a very popular garment. Lighter, silver, suspects cigarettes for the lighting of, classified issue, one per unit, *must* be returned to the station by 19.30 on operational day or lodged with P.C. Carter desk sergeant in the annex. All clear? Any questions?

JAMIESON: No, sir.

SIMON: None thank you, sir. One thing I don't get.

JAMIESON: Yeah?

SIMON: I mean, when we're off duty.

JAMIESON: Yeah.

SIMON: And we're caught short say . . .

JAMIESON: Uh huh.

SIMON: And we go into this convenience.

JAMIESON: Uh huh.

SIMON: I mean, how do we stop looking like members of the public who would not be averse to intimacy?

JAMIESON: Search me, squire. Just got to do our duty. Eh?

Play 'Wonderful World' by Herman and The Hermits.

Scene Three

A public lavatory. SIMON *enters. In uniform. After a while, enter* MAN. MAN's *eyes stray to* SIMON. MAN's *hands stray to* SIMON's *cock . . .*

SIMON: I should warn you that I am a police officer.

MAN: Sure.

SIMON: And I must warn you that anything you say will be taken down and used as evidence against you.

MAN: What's the hassle?

SIMON: And now I must ask you to remove your hand from my genitals.

MAN: What's got into you?

SIMON: I am a police officer.

MAN: You've never been like this before.

SIMON: I beg your pardon?

MAN: I said you've never been like this before.

SIMON: Listen you, I . . . What do you mean I've never been like this before?

MAN: You're usually such a lot of fun.

SIMON: Conceivably you are confusing me with someone else.

MAN: Maybe I am. You all look the same to me.

SIMON: And what do you mean by that?

MAN: You know, the gear. The old blue serge 'n' boot.

SIMON: Am I to understand that a person masquerading as a policeman uses these premises for sex?

MAN: I don't know about masquerading, he certainly comes in in uniform, usually about this time.

SIMON: From a theatrical costumier, I expect.

MAN: You do look awfully like him.

SIMON: Will you please remove your hand.

MAN: You're a real bundle of fun aren't you?

SIMON: You could get six months for this.

MAN: Listen.

SIMO: However, there is the question of Queen's evidence.

MAN: Oh, cut the queer jokes.

SIMON: Please. If you are prepared to turn Queen's evidence and help me trap this other criminal, I am prepared to forget all the charges.

MAN: Listen I don't . . .

SIMON: All you have to do is to stand by the urinal. Do not attract him by gesture, by voice or by expression but lead him to believe that you are a normal member of the public who would not be averse to homosexual practices.

MAN: Well, that is an accurate description of myself.

SIMON: Shut it. We haven't got much time. I will hide in the cubicle.

MAN: Listen, I don't want to get some poor sod –

SIMON: You do as you're told and there will be no trouble O.K.?

Enter HARRIS.

HARRIS: Evening all.

MAN: Police.

HARRIS: That's the one.

MAN: No, over there.

HARRIS: You what?

MAN: There's a policeman.

HARRIS: *Here's* a policeman.

MAN: I don't think you quite understand.

HARRIS: What's up with you today?

HARRIS *disappears beneath the level of the urinal.*

MAN: I don't think you've got this at all.

HARRIS: You what?

MAN: There's a policeman watching us.

HARRIS: Another one, great.

SIMON: I arrest you in the name of the law and I must ask you to accompany me to the station . . . Oh. Er . . . Sorry Sarge.

HARRIS: How many times have I told you, Simon? When will you ever learn?

SIMON: It's just that I . . .

HARRIS: How dare you interfere with a superior officer on the job?

SIMON: I thought that . . .

HARRIS: And what the hell are you doing here, any way?

SIMON: I was on my way home and I thought I'd nip in to see if . . .

HARRIS: To see if what?

SIMON: Suspects, Sarge. And I thought, anyway I wanted to go . . .

HARRIS: Listen Simon. For the moment I'll say nothing more about this. You're new to this lark. You're a bright enough lad, good marks from college. The sort of lad we're looking for. But watch it, son. Eh? And don't spend too much of your time hanging about public lavatories or you'll be in trouble.

SIMON: But Sarge – you're in here and? –

HARRIS: Listen son, I might be on duty might I not. I might be doing anything. It's not your duty to know what I'm doing. You work your way up through the section and you keep your nose clean and your mouth shut, right? Now clear off and we'll say no more about it. O.K.

SIMON: I'm just not . .

HARRIS: I'll deal with this merchant. You get back home to the wife and kids, eh? I take it you have got a wife and kids?

SIMON: Oh yes, sir. I mean, I plan to, sir.

HARRIS: Then you're in the clear aren't you? Eh? Now hop it.

SIMON: Yes sir . . . Good night.

HARRIS: Good night Simon. O.K.?

MAN: What's up with you lot?

HARRIS: You what?

MAN: What's up?

HARRIS: Search me, lad.

MAN: You're getting really confused. Muddleheaded, you know what I mean?

HARRIS, *after the* MAN *has gone, looks yearningly into the distance.*

Play 'Some Enchanted Evening.'

Scene Four

The office.

FEAVER: Come on in, Simon.

SIMON: Thank you, sir.

FEAVER: Sit down. Enjoying the work?

SIMON: Enormously, sir.

FEAVER: Good. What's the problem?

SIMON: It's just that –

FEAVER: Come on, lad, out with it.

SIMON: Why I came to you sir – is that I want it off the record.

FEAVER: Certainly, Simon.

SIMON: It's about a senior officer, sir.

FEAVER: I see.

SIMON: I have a complaint to make.

FEAVER: Who is the officer concerned?

SIMON: Sergeant Harris, sir.

FEAVER: Indeed. And what is the nature of your complaint?

SIMON: I am afraid, sir, that he may be using his privileged position in a way that is an abuse of trust, sir.

FEAVER: How do you mean, Simon?

SIMON: I think, sir, that he's . . . er . . . I think that he is a homosexual.

FEAVER: Do you know what you are saying, Simon?

SIMON: Yes, sir.

FEAVER: On what do you base this suspicion?

SIMON: Well, sir, I found him having oral sex with another man in a public convenience in the King's Road, sir.

FEAVER: Yes . . . and . . . ?

SIMON: Well, I mean – that led me to suppose that –

FEAVER: That what, Simon?

SIMON: That he might well be . . . er . . . homosexual.

FEAVER: How long have you been in the vice squad, Simon?

SIMON: Six weeks, sir.

FEAVER: And how long has Sergeant Harris been in the vice squad?

SIMON: Ten years I believe, sir.

FEAVER: And how long has Sergeant Harris been in the indecency unit?

SIMON: Eight years, sir.

FEAVER: Well then. Who is the more experienced man?

SIMON: Sergeant Harris, sir.

FEAVER: So don't you think he'd know if he were homosexual?

SIMON: I suppose so, sir.

FEAVER: Well then.

SIMON: Well then what, sir?

FEAVER: Don't you see how absurd your allegations sound?

SIMON: Not really, sir.

FEAVER: If what you say is true and can be proved we shall take it very seriously indeed. I'm going to hold a full and unprejudiced enquiry into this case, this is a very delicate area. And I want you to know, laddy, that if you have been touting a malicious rumour or making up tales to gratify some personal vendetta, you'll be in trouble. Attacks of this nature on the integrity of police officers are easy to make. Confidence in policing is as delicate and important a matter as faith in the Lord or in the fundamentals of mathematics. It is also very closely related to the needs and aspirations of society and to approach the problem with the ethical subtlety of, say, the Girl Guides (as some contemporary commentators do), is in my opinion crude and dangerous.

SIMON: Yes sir.

FEAVER: You may go now.

SIMON: Thank you sir.

FEAVER: Carry on.

SIMON: Can I say something, sir?

FEAVER: What?

SIMON: I came here, sir, because I believe we have to follow the book. We don't make the law, sir, and we're not above it and if we don't set an example then how can we expect people to follow it? That's all we need to worry about.

FEAVER: Did you understand a word of what I was saying just now?

SIMON: When, sir?

FEAVER: Never mind, laddy.

SIMON: Shall I go now, sir?

FEAVER: What sort of chap are you, Simon?

SIMON: How do you mean, sir?

FEAVER: Well what kind of person?

SIMON: Couldn't say, sir . . . Try to be . . .

FEAVER: Try to be what?

SIMON: I don't know, sir. Decent I suppose, sir.

FEAVER: Hard task.

SIMON: Sorry, sir?

FEAVER: Never mind.

SIMON: Is that all, sir?

FEAVER: Carry on, constable. I shall have your complaint looked into in good time and in good order.

SIMON: When will that be, sir?

FEAVE: It will be as soon as possible. We have to catch a few criminals as well as nobble coppers, you know. There are various complex departmental procedures to be gone through.

SIMON: Cut through bureaucracy, eh sir, weed out corruption to get at the truth.

FEAVER: You're red hot on corruption, aren't you, lad?

SIMON: Red hot, sir.

FEAVER: We all are at the moment. It's in the air. Clamping down. Quite a lot of people have been making personal telephone calls in office hours.

SIMON: Oh *no*, sir.

FEAVER: Seems incredible doesn't it? I blame television myself. Anyway your complaint is of a different order. It will be looked into.

SIMON: Thank you, sir . . . Sir?

FEAVER: What is it, Simon?

SIMON: I think I ought to tell you, sir, that I did make a personal telephone call. Last week, sir. In office hours.

FEAVER: Where to?

SIMON: Bristol, sir.

FEAVER: I see.

SIMON: I talked quickly, sir.

FEAVER: I appreciate your telling me this, Simon. For the moment we will let it pass.

SIMON: I expect the appropriate punishment, sir.

FEAVER: Simon, this is the police force not an establishment catering for sado-masochists.

SIMON: For what, sir?

FEAVER: *Carry on.*

SIMON: *Sir.*

FEAVER: Stone the fucking crows – where do they find them these days.

Play 'A Policeman's Lot is Not a Happy One' from The Pirates of Penzance.

Scene Five

The vending machine scene.

HARRIS: Evening, lad, tea?

SIMON: Evening, sir. Thank you, sir.

HARRIS: Everything O.K. on the squad?

SIMON: Fine, sir, fine.

HARRIS: There's a job on at Wimbledon. At 21.30. Code name Ganymede.

JAMIESONE: Common sir?

HARRIS: That's it.

JAMIESON: Disguise, sir?

HARRIS: You're not going, Jamieson. Simon's going.

SIMON: Sir.

HARRIS: Some of us on the squad feel it's time you got to know a few homosexuals, on the personal level.

SIMON: Sir.

HARRIS: Do you know any homosexuals?

SIMON: I don't think so, sir.

HARRIS: You don't sound too sure, lad.

JAMIESON: Sarge.

HARRIS: Jamieson.

JAMIESON: Sir.

HARRIS: You and Jamieson regular teamates aren't you?

SIMON: We rub along.

JAMIESON: This is it.

HARRIS: Well, as I said – we felt it was time for you to get to know a few members of the opposition. Find out their habits and so forth . . . You will approach the area by the 33 bus. On leaving the bus as inconspicuously as possible you will saunter towards the pond at the centre of the common in an assembled casual fashion. At 21.30 you will bury your Metropolitan Police equipment at the pre-arrranged spot A, and at 22.00 you will attempt to make reconnaissance contact with the targets agreed within the target zone.

SIMON: Sir.

HARRIS: You with me?

SIMON: I think so, sir.

HARRIS: You will of course be wearing the appropriate garments.

JAMIESON: Jock strap and football boots.

HARRIS: Very funny, lad, very funny. Now on this occasion we don't think it necessary to make an arrest.

SIMON: What do I do then, sir?

HARRIS: Talk, laddy. We want to know what the movements of the shirt-lifters are. If they plan any orgies. What they're getting up to. If they're involved in any new forms of sexual deviation. This type of thing. More tea?

Enter FEAVER.

FEAVER: What's this, a tea party?

JAMIESON: Would you like one, sir?

FEAVER: Yes please.

JAMIESON: We were discussing the under-cover operations, chief. Mingling with the opposition, sir.

FEAVER: Under cover-operations eh? Well . . . no . . . I'm not sure I approve.

JAMIESON: How do you mean, sir?

FEAVER: Don't get me wrong, Jamieson. I'm not expressing a disagreement with squad thinking on this one. But I'm not entirely sure the new ways are better than the old ways. Community policeman this and community policeman that. A policeman may be a member of a community but he's apart from it . . . don't you think?

SIMON: Living in police flats and so on, sir?

FEAVER: I don't know about living in police flats, laddy, I live in Putney and I don't advertise the fact that I'm in the force. I'm rather sensitive about it in fact . . . But I feel like a policeman, even in my pyjamas I feel like a policeman. You can't stop it can you? All the time it's ticking away like an unexploded TNT. You see a car parked on a double yellow and you say to yourself 'Right sonny, I'll have you'.

Enter WESTWICH.

WESTWICH: Quite right, Feaver and when you've got him give him everything you've got, right up the Kyber. Yes?

SIMON: Sir.

WESTWICH: Who's this?

HARRIS: Simon, sir. P.C. Simon recently seconded to this unit.

WESTWICH: Stand easy.

HARRIS: I'm sending him down to Wimbledon, sir, on Ganymede.

WESTWICH: Good, good. Does he know what to do?

HARRIS: Information and reconnaissance, sir. Very low profile.

WESTWICH: Quite. Who do we have on the ground on Wimbledon Common?

HARRIS: P.C. Porter, sir, but he's been very severely stretched.

WESTWICH: I'll bet he was . . . Keep in close touch with Porter, Simon. He's good on the ground, he's fast on his feet and I know of no better man on the squad as far as close shrubbery work is concerned? Where are you from?

SIMON: Basingstoke, sir.

WESTWICH: Is that in England?

SIMON: Yes, sir.

WESTWICH: Good. Welcome to the squad. You'll find the first few weeks a bit much but you'll soon get into the swing of it. Has he been down into the regions at all, Harris?

HARRIS: We will be sending him, sir.

WESTWICH: Good. Some very interesting new techniques being tried down in Bristol.

JAMIESON: The luminous trousers, sir.

WESTWICH: Don't be too clever for your own good, Jamieson.

FEAVER: We were discussing the changing face of police work, sir. The gently, gently approach as it were.

WESTWICH: No sense in making fun of it though, eh? Times move on and we must move with them, eh? Superintendent?

FEAVER: I suppose so, sir.

WESTWICH: Don't suppose, don't suppose. Remember that clothes convenience work, open space availability ploys, all these are the bread and butter of police work, but there's more to it than flaunting your Hampton on Wimbledon Common, laddy. Up here. Up here, the mind, intelligence, intelligence . . . How many men have we got into CHE, Harris?

HARRIS: Five, sir, full time and er one we're not too sure about.

WESTWICH: No?

HARRIS: Carter, sir. We think he may have gone over to the other side.

WESTWICH: Quite . . . another danger. Know your enemy, Simon but don't get to know him too well, eh?

SIMON: Right, sir.

WESTWICH: How about *Gay News*?

HARRIS: P.C. Harper is doing some book reviews for them, sir. They seem satisfied.

WESTWICH: What about?

HARRIS: Biography of Judy Garland, sir.

WESTWICH: No, what are they satisfied about?

HARRIS: They like his style, sir.

WESTWICH: Good. Harper is a keen young policeman who will go far. In three years he will probably be editing *Gay News* while you lot are still crawling around Hampstead Heath asking wellbuilt strangers for a light. Remember Intelligence. Intelligence. Nous. Carry on.

HARRIS: Sir.

WESTWICH: Best of luck with Ganymede, Simon.

SIMON: Sir.

WESTWICH: Anyone seen Doris with the trolley?

HARRIS: She was on the mezzanine, sir.

WESTWICH: Good. Good. Carry on, stand easy.

HARRIS: Right lad. 21.30 at the common. I've got to do my B.50's on gross indecency on one-man operated buses. Form for this, form for that. How we ever get anything done, I'll never know . . . Do you know, Division is talking about us taking over bestiality. Load of fucking alsatians and parrots all over the place. Vets taking statements – as if our case load wasn't heavy enough, eh, lad?

SIMON: Do people do it with parrots Sarge?

HARRIS: They do, lad, they do.

SIMON: How?

HARRIS: They get carried away.

JAMIESON: So do the fucking parrots. See you Sarge. He's a great officer.

SIMON: I don't know so much.

JAMIESON: How do you mean?

SIMON: Well . . . look . . . I think Sergeant Harris may be . . .

JAMIESON: May be what?

SIMON: A shirt lifter.

JAMIESON: Yeah?

SIMON: Yeah, a bender.

JAMIESON: Well, well, well this is what we find.

SIMON: Do you think he is?

JAMIESON: There's a lot of it about, John.

SIMON: I'm making a complaint about him.

JAMIESON: Who to?

SIMON: Chief Superintendent Feaver.

JAMIESON: Oh Feaver's an ace shirt-lifter, mate. Bent as a nine bob note. No problem. A one hundred per cent fully paid up fairy he is. It's backs to the walls where Feaver is concerned. Has he tried to get you to go into the long jump pits with him?

SIMON: No.

JAMIESON: Funny. You're not bad looking. Has he tried to get you to look at his train set?

SIMON: I didn't know he had a train set.

JAMIESON: He hasn't. But if he had it would have a *very* broad gauge. Know what I mean?

SIMON: No.

JAMIESON: Are you quite sure you're in the right department? You should be seeing the old ladies across the road, you should. Anyway – if Chief Superintendent Feaver offers to take you over the nine foot wall, tell him you like to tackle an assault course on yor own-io. Get my meaning?

SIMON: This is awful.

JAMIESON: It's life, mate. Life in the raw in the force. That's what you joined up for.

SIMON: Who can you trust around here?

JAMIESON: If you're talking about trust. Trust as trust. I reckon Commander Westwich. Top brass. He was here just now. We snap to it when he's on the scene, mush. Great man and a great copper. Trust him all the way . . . I'd go to hell and back for Commander Westwich if only they'd let me.

SIMON: How do you mean?

JAMIESON: You *know* . . .

He gets up.

Anyway mate, nice to have you on the squad. I'm off to Swan Lake.

SIMON: Is that on Wimbledon Common?

JAMIESON: Swan Lake, mush, is a ballet. They like ballet. Nous. Intelligence. Nous.

He turns and goes. SIMON *alone in the canteen. After a while a large* POLICE CONSTABLE *of hairy aspects enters pushing a trolly.*

P.C.: Fancy a rock cake?

He laughs lugubriously.

I'm Doris.

Scene Six

Music: 'The Dance of the Sugar Plum Fairy.' Lights up on WESTWICH's *flat. The* COMMISSIONER *is in informal clothes and reading a history of the Indian Wars. With him is* SHAW, *his manservant. The doorbell rings and we are into . . .*

The Dance of the Signets, from Swan Lake.

WESTWICH: Door, Shaw.

SHAW: Very good, sir. A young gentleman to see you, sir.

WESTWICH: Name of?

SHAW: Simon, sir. Police Constable Simon.

WESTWICH: Show him in.

SIMON: Evening, sir. Very sorry to disturb you, sir.

WESTWICH: You are?

SIMON: P.C. Simon, sir. Sorry to bother you at home.

WESTWICH: Not at all. That will be all, Shaw.

SHAW: Thank you, sir.

WESTWICH: Before you go, Shaw – will you take anything, Simon?

SIMON: A little whiskey would be most pleasant, sir.

WESTWICH: Glenmorangie, Shaw.

SHAW: Certainly, sir.

SIMON: Has he been with you long, sir?

WESTWICH: Since Aden.

SIMON: Fuzzy-wuzzies, sir, the Arabs.

WESTWICH: The land of the Koran.

SHAW *returns.*

Were you off duty afterwards?

SHAW: I was thinking of taking a short walk before retiring. Good, an old acquaintance of mine from the Horse Guards and I planned to walk in the direction of Green Park and . . .

WESTWICH: That will be all, Shaw. Now what exactly do you want to see me about?

SIMON: It's difficult to know where to begin, sir.

WESTWICH: I should begin at the beginning.

SIMON: Cheers. Two weeks ago I received concrete evidence that Sergeant Harris, Acting Instructor Grade One on the Indecency Unit, was, not to put too fine a point on it, sir, as bent as a corkscrew.

WESTWICH: I beg your pardon?

SIMON: And I believe that not only is Harris one of them, sir, but also Chief Superintendant Feaver, the man right beneath you sir, is a bit of a nancy boy on the quiet.

WESTWICH: Feaver? This is quite incredible, Simon.

SIMON: He doesn't look like one, does he sir? But this is it, I suppose. He has learnt how to disguise himself, sir.

WESTWICH: Where did you learn this?

SIMON: A very reliable constable, sir, in the department, whom I would not wish to name for fear of calling down recriminations on him, told me about Feaver being a bit of fruit, sir, and I actually caught Sergeant Harris with his . . .

WESTWICH: With his what, Simon. Say it!

SIMON: His . . . I can't, sir.

WESTWICH: How very disturbing for you. It does seem to disturb you frightfully. Have you told anyone else about this, Simon?

SIMON: Yes, I told Chief Superintendant Feaver about Harris, sir.

WESTWICH: And what did he say?

SIMON: He said he would look into it but I don't trust him, sir, that's why I've come to you, sir.

WESTWICH: What you're asking is difficult, you will appreciate that investigating this would be a question of Departmental politics.

SIMON: It's a question of justice, sir, isn't it?

WESTWICH: But even justice has to be administered, it doesn't just happen. You will appreciate that Feaver and his friends have in their turn some fairly powerful friends.

SIMON: Yes, sir.

WESTWICH: You will also appreciate that Chief Superintendant Feaver is a very long serving officer with a very fine record. He was the man who apprehended the Greek waiters. They had been through Llandudno Butlins like a knife.

SIMON: Well, sir . . . People have a right to know when other people are a bit . . .

WESTWICH: A bit what?

SIMON: You know, sir . . . a bit . . .

WESTWICH: A bit . . . musical?

SIMON: A bit twisted, sir.

WESTWICH: If I instigate an enquiry . . . well, it could jeopardise working relationships within the Department. But in your case, I think I feel I must take action.

SIMON: Thank you sir.

WESTWICH: You seem to me to be a very dedicated young man.

SIMON: Thank you, sir.

WESTWICH: I think you're probably a very fit young man.

SIMON: I suppose I am, sir.

WESTWICH: And a well-educated young man.

SIMON: Thank you, sir.

Pause.

WESTWICH: Do you like Houseman?

SIMON: I've never played, sir.

WESTWICH: No, no, no, Simon. Houseman's a poet. A very great poet.

SIMON: I'm afraid I didn't know that, sir.

WESTWICH: Houseman wrote some very beautiful poems.

SIMON: Thank you, sir.

WESTWICH: Yes. And just as the Greeks saw no shame in stripping, and, in 'agonies' or celebratory games, wrestling with each other, covered in linseed oil, so Houseman felt no shame in writing lyrics that are, in their quiet way, as frank as anything in the Greek Anthology. About youth.

SIMON: Yes, sir.

WESTWICH: What still alive at twenty-two?
A fine upstanding lad like you?

SIMON: Yes, sir, sorry, sir.

WESTWICH: That is a parody of Houseman, boy. And the parody of beauty is ugliness, shame and despair, which we, like Houseman, may shun but cannot always evade. I remember my old schoolmaster, Mr Chottin, approaching me and whispering 'Westwich Westwich – this is the Chinese torture' as he . . . twisted my sideburns like so . . . I thought he hated me but he didn't hate me. He hated himself for being old and sad and lonely while all around him the youths grew taller and taller and taller.

SIMON: Yes, sir.

WESTWICH (*not hearing*): In the full summer the eminent limes on the playing fields were as naked as hat racks to Mr Chottin. His heart was as bare as a Puerto Rican larder. All seasons were empty to him. And now that I am his age, I feel pity for the man and attempt to find beauty in what was then so clearly ugly and wrong. 'Begin afresh, afresh, afresh . . .' Is that Houseman or Larkin, boy?

SIMON: I'm not quite with you, sir.

WESTWICH: What was it Yeats said?

SIMON: Yeats, sir?

WESTWICH: He reminded us that love has pitched his mansion in . . . the place of excrement.

SIMON: In the toilet, sir?

WESTWICH: No. Do you know anything about beauty? I suppose you don't. You are a steward of excellence, Simon, beautiful and yet so innocent that sometimes when I look at you I see the ugly old man who taught me, stammering in the classroom, grey with the hots for what was then I suppose our innocence.

SHAW *enters and coughs.*

Ah, Shaw. You've returned.

SHAW: The barracks was closed, sir. I

think there is an emergency meeting in Northern Ireland, but I gather that there is something rather special going on at the coalhole tonight, sir.

WESTWICH: Yes.

SHAW: Is the young gentleman leaving, sir?

WESTWICH: Very shortly. I will sort out a possible line of procedure with someone very senior. I will be in total charge of the inquiry and if we win . . .

SIMON: Will we, sir?

WESTWICH: We'll have a jolly good stab at it.

SIMON: Yes, sir.

WESTWICH: Goodnight.

SIMON: Goodnight, sir. Goodnight, Corporal Shaw.

SIMON *goes*.

SHAW: This is boring, sir.

WESTWICH: What is.

SHAW: You know, sir. This business with Chief Superintendant Feaver again. We should stand together sir.

WESTWICH: Of course. Good order will be maintained. Nice lad.

SHAW: Very nice, sir. Not our type, I thought, sir. A bit neither carpet or hairbrush, if you see what I mean. – Coalhole?

Play 'I love you because you're you' by Jim Reeves.

Scene Seven

Lights up on FEAVER's office.

FEAVER: Is Commander Westwich in the canteen?

JAMIESON: He never uses it, sir. He goes to the Greek place across the road.

FEAVER: Will he be there now?

JAMIESON: I think he's in the building somewhere, sir.

FEAVER: He's not in his office.

JAMIESON: You've tried ringing him then, sir, have you?

FEAVER: I can't *ring* him. If I rang him it might look as if I wanted to talk to him.

JAMIESON: I thought you did, sir.

FEAVER: I do, Jamieson, but I don't want him to know I want to talk to him. I want to run across him casually. On the lifts or something.

JAMIESON: You could ride up and down in several lifts, sir. And hope he picked one of them.

FEAVER: I sometimes despair of you, Jamieson. Do you want to get on in this organisation?

JAMIESON: Er . . .

FEAVER: Maybe I could use Sergeant Hawkins.

JAMIESON: How do you mean, sir?

FEAVER: Is Sergeant Hawkins by the noticeboards?

JAMIESON: I . . .

FEAVER: Well find out, lad. Spy out the land for me. See if he's on the fifth floor.

Phone rings.

Answer that.

JAMIESON: Chief Superintendant Feaver's office. Who's speaking please? Detective Inspector Grubber. He says he's out on a job, sir. I mean he said he was out on a job. When he went, sir. A few moments ago. Yes. I mean no. No I couldn't catch him, sir. It was more than a few moments, it was. Yes . . . half an hour, sir. Right, sir. No, sir, I'm just manning the phones really, sir. Oh, right sir, thank you, sir. I'll tell him, sir. And I'll tell him that you've got the equipment for Holland Park, sir. Thank you, sir. P.C. Jamieson, sir. Yes, I am, sir. Well, I don't mind if I do, sir. Thank you very much, sir. Right you are then. No, no, no, sir, I haven't seen it. I saw the first one and then . . . bye then. Bye . . .

FEAVER: *Moron!*

JAMIESON: Sorry, sir.

FEAVER: Take the phone off the hook. I don't know about you, lad, I really don't. Do you think you can get through life by beaming like a goon at everyone and anyone.

JAMIESON: Do I beam like a goon, sir?

FEAVER: *I did not want to talk to D.I. Grubber!*

JAMIESON: Why ever not, sir?

FEAVER: Listen – Commander Westwich has taken over my enquiry into the business of Sergeant Harris. Why, I do not know. For all I know someone on the squad has been spreading malicious rumours about me. Will you massage my neck, Jamieson?

JAMIESON: You're the boss, boss.

FEAVER: Have people been spreading malicious rumours about me, Jamieson?

JAMIESON: About what, sir?

FEAVER: About me. Have people been saying that I'm . . .

JAMIESON: That you're what, sir?

FEAVER: That I'm not quite the thing. You know.

JAMIESON: Oh no, sir. People talk, sir. But in the nicest possible manner, if you see what I mean. I don't think any harm is intended.

FEAVER: I can't work out, Jamieson, whether you are incredibly devious or incredibly stupid.

JAMIESON: Probably a bit of both, sir.

FEAVER: Are you taking the piss, lad?

JAMIESON: I take the piss sometimes, sir. Do I not? I take life as it comes, sir. I try not to let it get me down. And I don't get mixed up with the politics, if you know what I mean.

FEAVER: You will in the end, laddie.

JAMIESON: As long as it isn't heavy politics, eh?

FEAVER: If certain people got to hear that I wasn't one hundred per cent 'how's your father' on certain issues, Jamieson, it could be very awkward for me. My daughter's just got engaged, you know.

JAMIESON: Terrific, sir.

FEAVER: To a very nice young lad called Brinkley. James Brinkley.

JAMIESON: Smashing, sir.

FEAVER: Apparently he's doing absolutely incredible things with the SDP.

JAMIESON: Nice for him, sir.

FEAVER: You're too bloody soft to make a good copper, Jamieson. You let too many things pass under your guard.

JAMIESON: I expect I'll turn stroppy about something one of these days, sir.

FEAVER: Could you . . . nip along to Commander Westwich's office and see if there are any memos lying around about this enquiry. He'll have written a memo to someone.

JAMIESON: Muggins lumbered again.

FEAVER: Go on, boy.

JAMIESON: I don't see what good all this'll do you, sir?

FEAVER: I might have to talk to some people. Hotchkiss of Venereal Planning is quite prone and I get on quite well with the Wrigley brothers. If I could put something together before the enquiry . . .

JAMIESON: I don't think it's entirely fair, sir. Why is it me who gets all the runaround to do with this, eh?

FEAVER: Because you're attached to my office, lad. If you come up with something we could nip over to the Greek restaurant at lunchtime and crack a bottle of retsina.

JAMIESON: Rave on! Hotchkiss, D.I. Grubber, Wrigley brothers, well, Fred anyway. Then there's Greenbaum and whatever he's got up his sleeve I'll be ready for him

Blackout.
Play 'Bang Bang' by Sonny and Cher.

Scene Eight

The court. An informal affair.

FEAVER: Proceed. You are Sergeant Peter Harris of V Division?

HARRIS: I am.

FEAVER: State how long you have been a member of the force.

HARRIS: Fifteen years, sir.

FEAVER: And of the Vice Squad?

HARRIS: Ten years.

FEAVER: And how long have you been

attached to the Indecency Unit with special responsibility for training and education?

HARRIS: Eight years, sir.

FEAVER: During this time have you ever engaged in such activity on or near a public lavatory in such a manner as to cause a breach of the peace?

HARRIS: I have not, sir.

FEAVER: Have you ever engaged in such activity in or near or adjacent to a public toilet in such a manner as liable to cause a breach of the peace in that toilet?

HARRIS: I have not, sir.

FEAVER: Have you, in fact, Sergeant Harris, ever been near a public lavatory in the time of your service to the Metropolitan Police Force except in so far as your professional duties took you to such a place?

HARRIS: I have not, sir.

FEAVER: May I enquire why not?

HARRIS: I believe that they are dirty, sir.

FEAVER: No more questions.

WESTWICH: Sergeant Harris, I want you to cast your mind back to the 22nd of September of this year.

HARRIS: If you wish.

WESTWICH: And I want you to tell the Court whether you were or were not in the public convenience on the corner of the Kings Road and . . .

FEAVER: I object, Commander Westwich, to this line of questioning. P.C. Simon's evidence has already been heard and . . .

WESTWICH: With respect, Chief Superintendant Feaver, I hope to prove that the accused was in the convenience referred to, not simply by reference to P.C. Simon's evidence but by the production of material proof that he did so. Exhibit A. Now when I bring on exhibit A, I am going to ask you if you recognise it, is that understood?

HARRIS: It is understood.

WESTWICH: Exhibit A. Now if we examine the exhibit. Now . . .

HARRIS: Yes, sir.

WESTWICH: Sergeant Harris, do you recognise the exhibit now before the Enquiry?

HARRIS: I . . .

WESTWICH: Do you?

HARRIS: It's . . . It is a door.

WESTWICH: Any particular kind of door?

HARRIS: I don't know, it could be a . . .

WESTWICH: Yes.

HARRIS: It could be a lavatory door.

WESTWICH: Do you recognise it, Sergeant?

HARRIS: I.

WESTWICH: Might you be able to say from which public convenience it comes?

HARRIS: I have never –

WESTWICH: Possibly a public convenience in the Chelsea area of London. Do you remember this, Sergeant . . . ? 'For a really good time telephone 01-733 8016.' Mmm?

HARRIS: I do not.

WESTWICH: How about 'I have a really good big one for any young lad in running shorts, make date.'

HARRIS: I do not recall ever having seen such a thing except as far as my professional duties took me.

WESTWICH: Let us speculate for a moment Sergeant. What sort of good time do you think I might obtain if I were to telephone 01-733 8016?

HARRIS: It would depend on who answered.

HARRIS: Sergeant, this is a very serious matter. Might I obtain homosexual satisfaction?

HARRIS: I . . . I don't know.

WESTWICH: Sergeant, I put it to you that the above mentioned telephone number is that of your own home and the good, big one referred to in the graffiti now before the Enquiry is, in fact, your own.

HARRIS: I utterly deny that I possess the item in question . . . or that I have ever advertised it in the manner in question.

WESTWICH: Very well. I should advise

the Enquiry that I have consulted a leading German Graphologist and that later we shall be hearing the evidence on the writing on the lavatory door. However, that may not be necessary.

FEAVER: May I enquire why not, sir?

WESTWICH: I propose to call Constable Jamieson.

FEAVER: Sir . . .

WESTWICH: Any objection?

FEAVER: None, sir.

WESTWICH: Step forward, Constable Jamieson. Now, Constable Jamieson, I want you to cast your mind back to a conversation you had by a vending machine eight days ago during which you informed P.C. Simon that Chief Superintendant Feaver was an ace shirt-lifter.

FEAVER: Objection, sir, you are leading the witness.

WESTWICH: In my opinion, witnesses usually need to be led. Now P.C. Jamieson, on what evidence did you make this allegation?

JAMIESON: I . . .

WESTWICH: Come along.

FEAVER: P.C. Jamieson, I must warn you that . . .

WESTWICH: That what?

FEAVER: That . . . nothing, sir.

JAMIESON: Well, sir, last June I went to Majorca.

WESTWICH: Yes?

FEAVER: I must protest. I cannot possibly see the relevance of P.C. Jamieson's holiday in connection with this enquiry.

WESTWICH: Well, shall we endeavour to discover the relevance?

JAMIESON: Where, as is my wont, I regularly bathed nude.

WESTWICH: Good. Why was this?

JAMIESON: In order to improve my physique, sir.

WESTWICH: Was this mixed bathing?

FEAVER: Jamieson, I must warn you . . .

WESTWICH: *Please, we will hear the evidence!*

JAMIESON: It was not, sir. It was men only, women were not permitted, sir.

WESTWICH: Did you see anyone from your place of work there?

JAMIESON: I . . .

FEAVER: I wish to formally record the fact that I am disgusted and appalled by that line of questioning.

WESTWICH: The Enquiry notes your objection. I repeat, did you see anyone from your place of work there?

JAMIESON: I did, sir.

WESTWICH: Can you point him out to this Enquiry?

JAMIESON *points to* FEAVER.

I ask the Enquiry to record that he is pointing at Chief Superintendant Feaver . . . and what was he doing, Constable?

JAMIESON: He was . . .

FEAVER: Must I listen to this?

WESTWICH: Does something tell you you may not enjoy it?

JAMIESON: He was engaged in a threesome, sir.

WESTWICH: What do you mean by that?

JAMIESON: He was having sexual intercourse with two Swiss travel agents, sir.

WESTWICH: Simultaneously?

JAMIESON: Well, almost simultaneously, sir.

WESTWICH: Congratulations, Constable. So far, may I say that you have given your evidence in a model fashion.

FEAVER: *But everything he has said has been a tissue of lies!*

WESTWICH: I made no reference to the truth of what Constable Jamieson has said, I simply wished to record that he said it in a convincing and charming manner. Now when the Chief Superintendant had finished with the Swiss travel agents did he not raise himself on his elbow and shout . . .

HARRIS: You can't do this to him, sir.

WESTWICH: I beg your pardon?

HARRIS: It will ruin his health, sir.

WESTWICH: Harris . . .

HARRIS: Confess, sir, that's the best thing, sir, confess.

WESTWICH: Harris.

HARRIS: Confess, sir, that's the best thing, sir, confess.

WESTWICH: Harris.

HARRIS: I admit everything, sir. Yes, yes, yes, yes. I and my accomplices in the force had love on the side from men we quizzed in vice probes. Sex was easy to come by in the 'live now, pay later' atmosphere of the clubs we frequented, masquerading as enemies of the porno exploiters, while, in fact, we were an integral part of 'Sleezy City', the sin capital of the EEC.

WESTWICH: Harris.

HARRIS: Whilst naming the guilty men in toilet dramas, we, and other top officials whose names I am not at liberty to disclose but up to and including C.S.I. Feaver and Sergeant Peter Harris, fifteen years on the force, both married men, resident in the Putney area of London, betrayed our vice squad colleagues in midnight . . . convenience capers. Cubicles certainly were engaged for lavatory love by the, no holds barred, officers who have a whole new meaning to the words, Mr Big.

WESTWICH: Harris, you have gone well over the top. Now sit down. Now, Feaver, having heard the evidence against you, have you anything to say?

FEAVER: I have been betrayed.

JAMIESON: This is it.

FEAVER: I have been stabbed in the back.

JAMIESON: I would say this is also true.

FEAVER: I have been treated with contempt and shame.

JAMIESON: Indeed, this is the case.

WESTWICH: Do you have any comment to make on the allegations against you?

FEAVER: I would just like to say that I have been twenty-five years on the force and nineteen of those have been spent with the Vice Squad. May I suggest that

prolonged explosure to vice in all its forms has unhinged me?

WESTWICH: Anything else?

FEAVER: I have no further statement to make at the present time.

WESTWICH: None?

FEAVER: None.

WESTWICH: You do not wish to refer to P.C. Jamieson?

FEAVER: Listen . . .

WESTWICH: You have nothing to say on the subject?

FEAVER: I . . .

WESTWICH: Mmmm?

FEAVER: Very good, sir. He will be relieved of all present duties and attached to your office.

WESTWICH: Excellent. Both of you are suspended for two weeks with privileges. But I would like to remind the Enquiry that this has not been a charade. I wish to draw the whole department's attention to the need for discretion at all times. Thank you.

All go except SIMON *and* JAMIESON.

SIMON: I don't get it.

JAMIESON: What?

SIMON: All that stuff about you.

JAMIESON: No?

SIMON: No.

JAMIESON: You will. He's really bent the rules for you.

SIMON: Yes?

JAMIESON: Sure. Look, the pressure on us cops at the moment is really something, mate. It's no joke being a Law Officer at the moment. Everyone tells us how to do our fucking job and it's the guys at the top who have to sort it. Now, a lot of bosses won't hold Enquiries like that these days. Everyone's too fucking paranoid. Rocks the boat. But he's really gone out on a limb for you. If any of this got any higher up he'd be in real trouble.

SIMON: But they were queers.

JAMIESON: God, you're really narrow minded, you are. I hope you thank the

Commander properly.

SIMON: You don't thank people for justice.

JAMIESON: I was always told to thank people for what they gave you and to say please if you want it.

SIMON: I had expected a severer punishment.

JAMIESON: Yeah?

SIMON: Yes.

JAMIESON: Where have you been all my life?

JAMIESON goes. Enter WESTWICH.

SIMON: Sir.

WESTWICH: Yes, Simon.

SIMON: Might I ask why you didn't . . .

WESTWICH: Why I didn't hit them harder?

SIMON: Yes, sir.

WESTWICH: No point. Everything has been satisfactorily resolved. They won't give you any more trouble. They are fundamentally a decent body of men.

SIMON: Yes.

WESTWICH: Don't worry.

SIMON: Er . . .

WESTWICH: And he wasn't too pleased about Jamieson, was he? Did you see his face . . . did you see it?

SIMON: I didn't quite understand what that was all about, sir.

WESTWICH: No? I thought about letting them off straight but that looks bad in the books, don't you agree? Anyway, my place next Friday, 10.00 o'clock.

SIMON: Oh yes, sir. Thank you, sir.

WESTWICH: Good boy.

SIMON: Sir . . .

WESTWICH: Yes, Simon, what is it?

SIMON: What will P.C. Jamieson do in your office, sir?

WESTWICH: The Hokey Cokey.

SIMON: Yes, sir . . . Good night, sir.

Play the Hokey Cokey.

ACT TWO

Scene One

Play 'More Than a Woman to Me.'

WESTWICH (*offstage*): Jamieson.

JAMIESON: Sir.

WESTWICH: Something a little more cheerful. Don't you think?

JAMIESON: I'll look out some Tamla Motown if that's all right Chief?

WESTWICH: I don't think I like Tamla Motown. Have we got any Philly Sound stuff?

JAMIESON: We've got some Reggae. How do you fancy Reggae?

Door bell.

WESTWICH: That'll be him.

SHAW: Shall I go, sir?

WESTWICH: Why not?

SHAW: In at the deep end, as it were.

WESTWICH: It is your *job,* Shaw.

SHAW: Carrying on duties, sir. (*He goes.*)

WESTWICH: I don't like reggae. What are the young people dancing to nowadays?

JAMIESON: We played the Three Degrees at Detective Inspector Haraway's leaving party.

WESTWICH: I have only confused memories of the occasion.

JAMIESON: It was a definitive night, sir.

Enter SHAW with SIMON.

SHAW: Gentlemen – Police Constable Simon.

WESTWICH: Good evening, Simon.

SIMON: Hello, sir.

SHAW: Constable Simon wishes to apologise for his late arrival. There was a person under his train at Victoria.

WESTWICH: Don't be so damn formal, Shaw.

JAMIESON: This is 'let your hair down' night.

WESTWICH: Quite. Now, Shaw, what can we offer the Constable?

SHAW: I bought in a few cases of Export Larger, sir. From our usual supplier.

JAMIESON: Brain Damage guaranteed.

SIMON: Do you have a dry white wine?

SHAW: I beg your pardon?

SIMON: Dry white wine. I'm watching my weight.

SHAW: I'm afraid we don't have any dry white wine, sir. At the moment. It's more a drink for the ladies, wouldn't you say?

JAMIESON: Give 'im a snowball.

All laugh.

WESTWICH: Don't tease the poor lad. Will lager beer suffice, Simon?

SIMON: Half a can.

SHAW: Half a can of lager. Very good, sir.

SIMON: I didn't know he was a Scottish soldier, sir.

JAMIESON: It was very sudden.

SIMON: What regiment is he from, sir?

WESTWICH: He tells everybody he was in the Signals, but I'm not an expert on uniforms.

SHAW *returns with the drink.*

SHAW: Funnily enough the Commander and I didn't meet in connection with military matters.

SIMON: Oh really?

SHAW: No, no, no. We met on the golf course, in fact. At the 19th hole.

WESTWICH: That is correct.

SHAW: The Commander has an absolutely remarkable forehand. And I am considered something of a marvel at getting out of bunkers. Do you like golf at all?

SIMON: Love it.

SHAW: But I expect you're the kind of player who gets most fun out of bashing the ball a hell of a long way. Aren't I right, sir?

WESTWICH: Corporal Shaw, I think I'd prefer a medium sherry. There's some in the fridge.

SHAW: It's South African, sir. Is that all right?

WESTWICH: We're moving on Corporal, but we haven't quite caught up with Peter Hain, yet.

All chuckle donnishly at this little sally. SHAW *goes.*

Now. Come over here, Simon.

SIMON: Thank you, sir.

WESTWICH: I expect you're fairly relieved it's all over.

SIMON: I'll say so, sir.

WESTWICH: Yes. (*Smiles.*) Sit down here.

SIMON: Thank you, sir.

WESTWICH: I was wondering, Simon . . .

SIMON: What, sir?

WESTWICH: Whether you were interested in walking at all?

SIMON: Oh I love it, sir.

WESTWICH: Because I'm going on a trip to the Black Mountains in Germany. Just me and a rucksack and a tent.

SIMON: Is Corporal Shaw going, sir?

WESTWICH: Not exactly. Corporal Shaw isn't the walking type. Are you, Shaw?

SHAW *has returned from the kitchen, followed them over and is now standing at the back of the sofa. He is drinking South African Amontillado sherry from a large pint mug in considerable quantities.*

SHAW: Can't stand walking. Can't abide it.

WESTWICH: Quite. And I was looking for someone . . .

SHAW: To walk with.

WESTWICH: Quite.

SHAW: Someone to walk with, someone to talk with.

SIMON: I'd have to see if I can afford it, sir.

WESTWICH: Oh quite. Do you have a flat-mate?

SIMON: I'm living with a young man from Lloyds Bank at the moment, sir.

WESTWICH: Excellent. I hear they're a very reliable organisation.

SHAW: I'm in favour of the Commander doing it. Aren't I Commander? I think it's right up your street. I'm getting too old for walking. If you want to go walking, and that's what I say to the Commander, you go walking with a younger man, an altogether younger man than I am, don't I Commander?

WESTWICH (*bored*): Yes.

SHAW: Yes?

WESTWICH: Corporal Shaw, go easy on the sherry.

SHAW: Don't worry about the sherry, sir. Plenty more sherry in the fridge. Plenty more sherry in the hall.

SIMON: I'd love to come, sir, if it's walking and outdoor things. I'm sure I could afford it.

SHAW: I thought you would. (SHAW *comes round the corner of the sofa and sits next to them, very closely*.) You'll have such fun. By the day the hot baking hillsides and at night it's slip into the sleeping bag under the stars. If there's anything I like it's slipping into a sleeping bag under the stars.

SIMON: Whereabouts in Germany are the Black Mountains, sir?

WESTWICH: In the south, I think.

SHAW: Nicest part, don't you think?

SIMON: I don't know Germany very well, I'm afraid.

SHAW: It's where the Nazis started. Remember the Nazis?

SIMON: I'm afraid I don't.

SHAW: Very good long jumpers, the Nazis.

WESTWICH: Why don't you look after the other guest, Corporal?

SIMON: Is there another guest, sir?

JAMIESON: What do you think I am, a house breaker?

SIMON: If you and the Corporal want to talk privately, sir I'll just . . .

SHAW: Never interfere between an NCO and a Senior Officer, eh Simon? Quite right.

WESTWICH: Do stay, the Corporal is just leaving.

SHAW *gets up*.

SHAW: Oh, I'm always just leaving, aren't I? I'm always given the bleeding elbow, I am, aren't I? I'm always just on the way to the fucking door.

WESTWICH: For God's sake, man.

SHAW: I'm sorry, sir. I must have my say.

WESTWICH: Shut up!

SHAW (*grinning at* SIMON): What's the matter with you, sonny? (*Menacing.*) Scared? What are you scared of? You're sailing fucking close to the wind to be scared, aren't you? What's to be scared of with old Shaw?

WESTWICH: For God's sake, man. Stop it.

SHAW: Will you stop it? (*Pause.*) I'm pissed off with it, if you want to know, fucking pissed off with it. Who goes round Lipton's with the fucking trolley? It isn't you, is it? Who makes sure we've got the meat for Wednesday and the cabbage for Thursday? Is it you? Fucking isn't. All I require is a little bit of acknowledgement. In any decently run organisation I would have received enough of it already.

SIMON: Oh Jesus Christ!

SHAW: Oh, do me a favour! One more minute of this wide-eyed, blue-eyed boy act and I'll throw up, I really will.

SIMON: Oh Jesus Christ, I didn't . . .

SHAW (*getting closer to* SIMON *and prodding him in the chest*): Now just you remember.

WESTWICH: Shaw, for God's sake, man, get control of yourself.

SHAW: Control of yourself, control of yourself. You've got control of me, sir. Hoovering, hoovering, who moves the Junior Deluxe Hoover round the carpet? Is it him? No way is it him. Who makes sure he gets clean shirts? The woman next door? Not on your sodding life.

He's backed SIMON *right up against the wall.* SIMON *is terrified.*

Well, use your nous, lad. How else do you think we spend our evenings in the armed forces? It's a man's life in the regular army, or haven't you read the adverts? (*Very angry.*) And I've seen lads like you before. Fly as you like. Sail as close to the fucking wind as you want to. I know your little game, sonny, right from the word go.

SIMON: I am going.

WESTWICH: Stay where you are! Corporal Shaw is in breach of orders. He is letting the side down.

SIMON: I'm sorry, sir.

WESTWICH *still has the authority of the unit over* SIMON. *Pause.*

I'm just not with this.

WESTWICH: You're with it, Simon. Now, once again, about this holiday . . .

SIMON: Look . . . I'm not going anywhere with you. . . . you twisted sod . . . twisted bent bunch of sods. (*Moving away towards the door.*) There are honest coppers. I'm off to find one.

WESTWICH: Just you remember this: Any place you go into, every single time you move outdoors, we'll be watching.

SIMON: Like I said, there are honest coppers. (*He goes.*)

WESTWICH *smiles at him sadly*.

JAMIESON: Well, well, this is what we find. Perhaps we could send him on a course?

WESTWICH: It's too late for that. Something will have to be done.

Play – 'Move over Darling' by Doris Day.

Scene Two

Enter BREEN, *then the two officers,* HARRIS *and* JAMIESON *follow on after* SIMON.

JAMIESON: What'er you getting? Nice day.

HARRIS: F8 and screw the shadows.

JAMIESON: Okey dokey.

SIMON *peeing.*

BREEN: Don't think I've seen you in here before.

Pause.

SIMON (*with a great deal of paranoid distrust*): I expect you're not averse to a wee bit of the old hokey cokey, eh?

BREEN: What *are* you talking about?

SIMON: I'm sure you're the world bloody expert on broad gauge railway trains, right?

BREEN: I fail to understand why –

SIMON: Well *mate*, as soon as I've finished this, I shall be off, mate. I won't be waiting around.

BREEN: Fine.

SIMON: OK?

BREEN: Fine.

SIMON: Left your cravat at home did you?

BREEN: I'm afraid I don't possess a cravat . . .

SIMON: No?

BREEN: No.

SIMON: How about rings?

BREEN: Sorry?

SIMON: Do you like . . . rings at all?

BREEN: Not much. I find them a bit effeminate, actually.

SIMON: Yes?

BREEN: Yes.

SIMON: It's amazing isn't it? To what lengths you lot will go to hide it.

BREEN: To hide what?

SIMON: Oh, don't try and pull the wool over my eyes, sunshine. I wasn't born yesterday. I'm not the naive prat some people take me for.

Pause. Realises who it is.

Oh my God, it's Roger Huskey!

BREEN: Sorry?

SIMON: Hello, many dinners in the oven?

BREEN: What?

SIMON: The TV series. In real life you look like you are a poof.

BREEN: Thanks a lot.

SIMON: Actually, these days I'm seeing them everywhere. I thought the Archbishop of Canterbury might be one the other day. I'm going demented.

BREEN: You certainly seem a little –

SIMON: But Roger Huskey! And I thought

you was a poof! I mean you look like a bloody poof if you'll excuse my French.

BREEN: It's probably direct light. It's notoriously unflattering.

SIMON: I'm most terribly sorry. I have to be rather careful in public lavatories.

BREEN: Really?

SIMON: Oh yes, I didn't really want to come in here.

BREEN: No?

SIMON: But I just cracked, you know.

BREEN: I know.

SIMON: Really boring, that's the way it goes. I do admire your series.

BREEN: You do?

SIMON: You're so natural.

BREEN: Well, thank you.

SIMON: That bit when you got Mary out of the caravan.

BREEN: Mmm.

SIMON: Terrific.

BREEN: Thanks.

SIMON: And you do all your own stunts, right?

BREEN: I do.

SIMON: Incredible.

BREEN: Cigarette?

SIMON: Not here, if you don't mind?

BREEN: Perfectly safe.

SIMON: I suppose it is. I keep seeing police around every door. And I thought you might be a . . .

BREEN: A what?

SIMON: Oh, it doesn't matter. Jesus, Roger Huskey!

BREEN: Clem Breen's my real name.

SIMON: Hi, Clem, most people just call me Simon. Simple Simon.

BREEN: Hi.

Pause.

SIMON: Tell me, Clem, I hope you won't think this is a personal question, but you and Mary . . .

BREEN: Yeah?

SIMON: You were together for six years, wasn't it?

BREEN: That's right.

SIMON: And you're both Virgos. And I mean, what happened?

BREEN: Ooh . . . old problem.

SIMON: Sure.

BREEN: I just had to come to terms with myself.

SIMON: My favourite one was the one where Mary pretended she had a paralysed leg, you remember?

BREEN: Oh sure.

SIMON: Because Dr Strackham was running this clinic and hiding the drugs in the bedframes.

BREEN: Mmm.

SIMON: And when she came in like that, oh, it was so funny, you know . . .

BREEN: I remember.

SIMON: And it had an awfully good last scene.

BREEN: Because she was hobbling like that around the room.

SIMON: You came up around her and put your . . . oh, it was great . . . the way you two acted together, you could always tell, you were husband and wife, you know.

BREEN: Er . . . I know.

SIMON: If you don't mind, one at a time, this toilet's engaged. (*Suddenly laughing.*) I loved the one in the Lake District, too.

BREEN: I remember it well.

SIMON: You had this row when she'd broken her arm rock climbing, do you remember?

BREEN: Mmm.

SIMON: And she came up to you with her arm in a sling like this, and you opened your –

BREEN *grabs* SIMON *and they kiss.* SIMON *struggles.* HARRIS *and* JAMIESON *come out of the stalls, filming them, snapping, sound recording, the lot.*

BREEN: Oh, bloody hell!

HARRIS: Nicked you again, laddy.

BREEN: In and out of the fucking houses. What a waste of your and my time, isn't it?

JAMIESON: Listen, mate. We've got a job to do, you've got a job to do, that's the way it is. Shall we all try to be a little bit pleasant about this?

SIMON: Pleasant, pleasant, what the fuck is this?

JAMIESON: Now you, you really are a pervert. A policeman on duty. You'll get a fucking suspension! I'm ashamed of you, Simon, I really am.

BREEN: Well, shall we get down to the station. I've got to be at Heathrow at 9.00 o'clock.

HARRIS: Steady as you go, steady as you go. It's this lad we want to talk to. Mr Breen, you and I have met before. I think we can describe ourselves as old adversaries. But, I think both of us would agree that there is nothing so despicable as a bent copper, and that's what we're looking at here.

SIMON: Bent copper! I like that. Who's fucking bent? It's you lot that's bent, all of you. (*To* BREEN:) You and all!

BREEN: I'm not bent, mate. I'm just out for a night's entertainment. And if I fancy it, why shouldn't I? For Christ's sake . . .

SIMON: Fucking funny place for a night out.

BREEN: Well, you didn't have to come in here, did you?

SIMON: I wanted to go. I was desperate.

BREEN: So was I.

SIMON: Maybe – but we weren't desperate for the same thing, were we?

BREEN: Speak for yourself.

SIMON: Look, what you were going to do is disgusting.

BREEN: Well, what you were planning to do isn't exactly number one spectator sport across the nation, is it?

SIMON: Sex should be beautiful.

BREEN: Well, in that case you should be very glad to run across it in a public convenience.

JAMIESON: Come along with me, then. I'll show you to your cell. OK? By the way, Roge, love the show.

JAMIESON gives BREEN a broad and suggestive wink.

BREEN: At last someone with a sense of humour. Come on, then – it's ages since I had a policeman.

JAMIESON: Really?

They leave together. WESTWICH *enters.*

WESTWICH: You see, Simon?

SIMON: I see.

WESTWICH: Doesn't pay, does it?

SIMON: What doesn't?

WESTWICH: Still time.

SIMON: Go screw yourself!

WESTWICH: I think you probably really are a pervert. I can hardly wait. Sergeant! Get this lad down at the station on a D-50.

HARRIS: Sir!

SIMON: Don't touch me.

HARRIS: I wasn't intending to. Move! At the double.

HARRIS *and* SIMON *leave.* SIMON *marching double time, knees up.* WESTWICH *inspects one of the stalls.* JAMIESON *enters.*

WESTWICH: Where is Mr Breen, Jamieson?

JAMIESON: In the van, Chief.

WESTWICH: Has he entrusted you with a letter, Jamieson?

JAMIESON: It's his autograph, sir.

WESTWICH: You seemed to take an age.

JAMIESON: He was pointing out an aspect of the facade, sir. Apparently it was designed by somebody or other.

WESTWICH: Well, I suppose it was, Jamieson. I don't suppose it fell off a lorry.

JAMIESON: No, sir.

WESTWICH: Do you have any interest in art, Jamieson?

JAMIESON: I quite liked the book you gave me, sir. The first bit.

WESTWICH: Yes?

JAMIESON: But I can't get along with the cubists. I can't see eye to eye with that at all.

WESTWICH: No?

JAMIESON: Take Picasso.

WESTWICH: Yes.

JAMIESON: Starts OK, then goes off the rails. Square people. I ask you. Ridiculous.

WESTWICH: What will they think of next?

JAMIESON: Don't get you, sir.

WESTWICH: Cigarette?

JAMIESON: Thought you'd given up.

WESTWICH: I just started again.

JAMIESON: Stunt your growth.

They smoke.

WESTWICH: Do you know there's a champagne bottle in there?

JAMIESON: Get away! Anything in it?

WESTWICH: 'Fraid not. They have a high old time, the chaps we pinch, don't they?

JAMIESON: Oh they do, sir. They live at a fair old pace.

WESTWICH: I was expelled from my school, Marshdale, you know.

JAMIESON: Yes, sir?

WESTWICH: Little adventure with a junior boy. Third Form was warned about me. But, when I went up before the beak I didn't bleat or mutter or apologise. I took my medicine like a man.

JAMIESON: I bet you did, sir.

WESTWICH: Queer. Always been a little queer. But I don't bloody advertise the fact.

JAMIESON: Roge is very extreme, sir.

Pause.

WESTWICH: Look, if we all rushed around advertising the fact, what would become of order? It might suit hairdressers, Jamieson, but it wouldn't do for us, would it?

JAMIESON: I wouldn't have thought so, sir.

WESTWICH: Take the army. Tons of fags in the Army. But discreet. Yes? You don't see platoon after platoon nancying past the Queen, hardly able to keep their hands off each other. For God's sake, once you allow the thing to slide then you do bloody slide all the way down, no end to it, madness, formlessness.

JAMIESON: All I was saying was, though, Chief, they have a good time.

WESTWICH: Yes, but, do what you like, where you like but don't brag about it and don't frighten the bloody horses. Home sweet home.

Play 'Night Moves' by Bob Seger.

Scene Three

Wimbledon Common. Night. HARRIS and JAMIESON are viewing with binoculars. A tense, hard-working atmosphere prevails. Also a total absence of dingle.

JAMIESON: I can't get anything at all on Queensmere.

HARRIS: The little bastards are quiet tonight.

JAMIESON: It's been raining, sir. They don't like bad weather.

HARRIS: I don't know so much. I've had some incredible results in late November. They seem to get worked up just before Christmas.

JAMIESON: I'm getting something in Sector Z.

Peering.

These night sight bins are a bit naff, Sarge.

HARRIS: They're Japanese. (*Gloomily.*) Do you remember Operation Rimmer, lad?

JAMIESON: Can't say as I do, Sarge.

HARRIS: Fellow called Pitchmore built it. Down the workshops. Real DIY merchant, if you take my meaning. It was a fully operational urinal built out of laminated plastic, squawk button in every cubicle, plus electrically operated grille. When the thing was at maximum capacity – red light went on, grille shut down and the whole caboodle shot off across the Thames at 20 knots. We nicked thirteen men in twenty-four hours.

Enter WESTWICH.

JAMIESON: Evening, sir.

WESTWICH: Evening. All well?

JAMIESON: Activity in Sector Z, sir.

WESTWICH: Oral intercourse?

JAMIESON: Buggery, sir. As far as I can make out.

WESTWICH *takes a look.*

WESTWICH: Neither one thing nor the other as far as I can see. Where are Hawkins and the hand to hand mob?

HARRIS: They went back up to the village, sir.

WESTWICH: It's infernally quiet, don't you think? What's happened to their libidos, for God's sake!

JAMIESON: It's so easy to get laid these days, sir.

WESTWICH: I *beg* your pardon, Jamieson?

JAMIESON: Discos, pubs, gay holidays, gay cookery classes, gay dating agencies. Who needs to prowl around Wimbledon Common getting their arses frozen off.

WESTWICH (*with a sense of the importance of his mission*): We do. Apparently.

JAMIESON: Quite, sir.

WESTWICH: But our job, Jamieson, is to get on and do what we're told without asking too many damn fool questions.

HARRIS: Shirt-lifter at nine o'clock, sir.

WESTWICH: Where? Where?

HARRIS: Coming our way, chief.

JAMIESON: I've clocked him. Twenty-five yards. Closing fast.

WESTWICH: Well, shall we move, gentlemen? Shall we get to work?

HARRIS: Yes, sir!

They get down in cover. Enter SIMON.

SIMON: Pssst!

Pause.

Pssst!

WESTWICH: Whom do you think this is designed to attract?

JAMIESON: Grass snakes, I should think, sir.

SIMON: Pssst!

Pause.

Sex anyone?

Pause.

Cock fun?

They're not reacting in any way. Just watching closely.

HARRIS: What the hell is he playing at?

JAMIESON: Perhaps our young friend has seen the light . . .

WESTWICH: Anything's possible, Jamieson.

JAMIESON: Not that little charmer.

WESTWICH: Maybe he wants to find out what it's like.

SIMON *loiters unconvincingly. Practises what he thinks are the right mannerisms.*

JAMIESON: Perhaps he wants to look convincing when the great day comes.

WESTWICH: Which of us can lay his hand on his heart and say he has never rehearsed his sexual overtures?

JAMIESON: Me.

SIMON: Right you bent bunch of bastards. This is your usual beat is it not? And Simple Simon's here before you. I'll find out what you get up to.

HARRIS: What on earth does that lad imagine we get up to out in the field. It's my feeling he needed more than a D.50, sir. Banning him from the building for two weeks wouldn't do it. He needs –

WESTWICH: He couldn't keep away, could he? (*Still stuck on him.*)

HARRIS: What's the next move, sir?

WESTWICH: I shall approach him.

JAMIESON: This is serious, sir.

WESTWICH: It's like a cry for help. Don't you think? The poor lad could have gone off and joined Tesco's by now. But he can't keep away. Look at him. Like a rabbit in the headlights.

JAMIESON: Sir –

WESTWICH *crosses to* SIMON.

WESTWICH: Good evening, Simon.

SIMON: Oh!

HARRIS *and* JAMIESON *reveal themselves.*

Oh!

WESTWICH: Well? What were you hoping to find? Me?

Pause.

Him? Us?

Pause.

Or . . .

JAMIESON: Yourself.

SIMON: *Don't think I don't know what goes on when you're on manoeuvres! You're at it all the time, aren't you? You're insatiable!*

WESTWICH: Simon – this is an exercise. We are on the job. OK? But there is a place for leisure.

Watching him.

My place. Next Friday. Nine o'clock. OK?

SIMON: I don't want to spoil my chances, sir, do I?

JAMIESON: Come on in to Bird's Eye country . . .

WESTWICH: *Jamieson!*

HARRIS: Everything OK, sir.

WESTWICH: I knew you'd see sense in the end. Now, it's freezing cold out here. Why don't you ask the constable to recommend you a pleasant hostelry where you can meet some of your sort of person.

JAMIESON: They serve lizards up at the Green Man.

WESTWICH: *Please!*

Pause.

Carry on!

They leave. SIMON *alone.*

SIMON: *Think you've talked me down, do you? Well you haven't! I'm still in with a chance, mate!*

Pause.

I'll come to your party and I'll sort you out. I swear I will.

Play 'Big John.'

Scene Four

The Second Act party scene.

Lights up on SHAW *holding a tray of canapes. Then into the scene.* HARRIS, FEAVER *on stage.*

FEAVER: Does anyone know what this party is in aid of?

HARRIS: The crime figures have just been released. Apparently there's been an eight per cent drop in buggery and oral intercourse is almost in single figures.

FEAVER: Don't I know it!

Pause.

But is it us, Sergeant? Or is it something else? The Falkland crises? The weather? One doesn't know.

Enter WESTWICH.

WESTWICH: It's us, Feaver, make no mistake about it. If we weren't on the job, we'd have runaway buggery, you mark my words. Faith in one's profession's relevance to the rest of society must be maintained and celebrated in spite of any evidence to the contrary adduced by the laity. Now – what's the film show?

HARRIS: Tunisian days, sir.

WESTWICH: Excellent. Is it good?

FEAVER: I believe the dog is very good, sir.

HARRIS: And I've hired some takeaway Chinese, sir.

WESTWICH: Excellent. What are their names?

HARRIS: Wong? Wing?

WESTWICH: Your pronounciation is exquisite, Sergeant.

FEAVER: And Constable Jamieson came on hot and strong in the Entertainment's Committee so we hit on something –

Doorbell.

FEAVER: That'll be him, now.

WESTWICH: Door, Shaw.

SHAW: Very good, sir.

He goes. Re-emerges with JAMIESON *as Liza Minnelli.*

WESTWICH: Very good!

FEAVER: Thank you, sir.

WESTWICH: Uh?

FEAVER: It was my idea, sir.

HARRIS: If the real Barbra Streisand walked in now, you wouldn't know the difference, would you, sir?

ALL: *Liza Minnelli, Sarge!*

WESTWICH: That wig is most becoming, Jamieson.

JAMIESON: Thanks, sir. My mum made it for me.

WESTWICH (*watching him*): You bring back memories of my favourite European city before they built that frightful fence. Are you going to sing later?

JAMIESON: If this corset hasn't done for my bollocks by then.

WESTWICH: We shall expect coloratura.

Doorbell.

Door, Shaw.

SHAW: You sure you wouldn't like to get it, sir?

WESTWICH: *Door.*

He turns and sees SIMON as Liza. Pause.

Oh!

Enter SIMON. He too is dressed as Liza Minnelli.

Oh – very, very, very good.

SIMON: Well, I thought – you know, I mean, I had a think – I decided I was being a bit of a prude . . . it's only a bit of fun, isn't it – right?

WESTWICH: Right.

SIMON: I mean, at the end of the day, what does it matter.

HARRIS: Well done, lad.

SIMON: I think I've had an Oedipus complex.

ALL: No . . .

SIMON: I think so, I think that was it.

ALL: No.

SIMON: No, no, no – I'm a regular brown hatter – always have been, always will be – I've got a dress on, and knickers, and a bra, and nylons, and a roll-on pantie girdle.

WESTWICH: You've certainly done the job thoroughly.

SIMON: Well, this is it. If you're going to be a poof – do it properly. Right?

WESTWICH: Oh, right.

Pause.

I adore people with obvious natures. Simplicity is very high on my list of priorities.

SIMON: Oh good.

HARRIS: Film show, film show. This way to the stalls.

FEAVER: And can we *not* try to trip over the wires as we go through. The projector is nicked from Central Services OK?

ALL: Hooray!

HARRIS: Take your seats, gentlemen, please.

JAMIESON: I'll be your best man.

FEAVER: Come along, lad. Come along.

They go.

SHAW: Will you be with us for the film, sir?

WESTWICH: Later.

SHAW: Very good, sir.

He goes.

WESTWICH: So. Here we are.

SIMON: At last.

WESTWICH: At last.

SIMON: How about . . . we move away from here and commit an offence?

WESTWICH: What kind of an offence?

SIMON: A punishable offence, sir.

WESTWICH: Good, good.

SIMON: I really feel like a bit of gross indecency.

WESTWICH: Oh, me too.

SIMON: Give it to me with your big cock.

WESTWICH: Yes, of course, of course. Er . . . do you want me to say anything? You haven't got anything in that braziere have you?

SIMON: No, no. Only a pair of hard nipples waiting to respond to your probing fingers, sir. I want your proud organ to enter me like a train, sir.

WESTWICH: Yes.

SIMON: Well – go on. It's your turn.

WESTWICH: My turn to what?

SIMON: To talk.

WESTWICH: What do I say?

SIMON: I don't know. You've had more experience at it than me. What do you usually say when someone says to you 'Give it to me with your big cock'?

WESTWICH: It depends whether I'm on duty, or how much I've had to drink, or how I feel. I do have feelings. I might say *'eheu fugaces postume labuntur anni necpietas mori'*.

SIMON: What does that mean, sir?

WESTWICH: It's Latin.

SIMON: Is it Latin for 'Yes, I will give it to you with my big cock'.

WESTWICH: No, I'm afraid not.

SIMON: Oh, you're a bit slow aren't you?

WESTWICH: It's your seduction technique. I find it disconcerting.

SIMON: Let's start again.

WESTWICH: Certainly.

SIMON: Look – you say – 'I want you to come into my hard back'.

WESTWICH: I'm not a publisher.

SIMON: Say 'Bury your tongue in my proud white arse'.

WESTWICH: No.

SIMON: Well, say something.

WESTWICH: Very well. I think you're frightfully attractive.

Enter SHAW.

SHAW: All going well, sir.

WESTWICH: Perfectly.

SHAW: I'm going to stand the men down.

WESTWICH: Excellent.

SHAW: And start the film show.

WESTWICH: Good. Very well, Simon. I want to nibble your cock, OK?

SIMON: Great, sir.

WESTWICH: Now shall we get down to it, Simon?

SIMON: Certainly, sir. I just have to go to the bathroom.

Enter JAMIESON.

JAMIESON: Where's he off to then?

WESTWICH: God knows.

JAMIESON: Coming across then, is he?

WESTWICH: That's the impression I gained.

JAMIESON: You're a fucking perve sometimes, sir.

WESTWICH: Am I? Well – he is a bit of a monster.

JAMIESON: Frankenstein had a monster, and look what happened to him.

WESTWICH: Look what happened to the monster.

JAMIESON: He's taking his time.

WESTWICH: He is.

JAMIESON: Maybe he's turning back into a pumpkin.

WESTWICH: God knows. I don't know why I bother, really. I can't ever see him making a policeman.

JAMIESON: How's the file on him, sir?

WESTWICH: He's committed almost every known deviation within the last fortnight. According to the file. Mind you, sometime's one's junior officers are a little over-zealous. I think it's time I took the squad in hand a little.

JAMIESON: I see, sir.

WESTWICH: And it's time you took yourself in hand, laddy. You won't get on in this outfit by lounging around in suspenders and tights in the flats of senior officers; promotion isn't simply a matter of who you know, Jamieson. It's where you're at.

JAMIESON: Berlin, sir. 1936.

WESTWICH: *Oh, for God's sake, man!*

He storms off. JAMIESON alone on stage begins to sing a Liza Minnelli number. Fade to black on whatever he chooses to sing . . . Preferably 'Bye, bye mein liebe herr'.

Scene Five

Lights up on FEAVER and HARRIS alone with the stage set as per The Enquiry in Act One.

FEAVER: I've had a long and detailed letter of complaint from London Zoo.

HARRIS: I must tell you, quite frankly, sir, I can't take it any more. I haven't had a weekend off in two years. Sex, sex, sex. That's all anyone in this department ever thinks about. Frankly, sir, I'd rather have a boiled egg and a cup of tea.

FEAVER: That's not what I hear from the keeper of the small mammal house.

Enter WESTWICH, SIMON, HARRIS.

WESTWICH: Now, gentlemen, I hope this won't take more than a few minutes. We are here to consider the D.50 on P.C. Simon with reference to an offence committed with one R. Huskey on the 22nd of September of this year, and may I say that since this order was carried out your attitude towards the squad has improved a great deal.

SIMON: Has it?

WESTWICH: I think so yes.

Enter JAMIESON.

FEAVER: You are late, constable.

JAMIESON: Transvestite tuperware party, Ealing.

WESTWICH: I intend to take this opportunity to make some more general remarks about the state of the squad.

FEAVER: Sir?

WESTWICH: What is it, Feaver?

FEAVER: I think you ought to know, sir, that at your flat on Tuesday last, the accused illegally taperecorded a passage of conversation between yourself and him, sir.

HARRIS: Not only did he tape it but he paid a typist to transcribe it, sir.

SIMON: You bastards, you've stolen that.

FEAVER: I considered it my duty, bearing in mind, sir, whatever departmental disputes arise from time to time, sir, we're fairly clear where our loyalties lie.

SIMON: You bastards . . .

HARRIS: We are not in the habit of going behind the backs of superior officers.

FEAVER: Would you like me to play the tape, sir?

WESTWICH: I am supposed to have said this and if I did, then I don't think I need to hear them, and if I did not, then the same applies.

FEAVER: Yes, sir.

WESTWICH: Constable Simon, this is very serious. What did you intend to do with this material?

SIMON: Take it to someone very senior from another department and on the *Daily Mail.*

ALL *fall about laughing.*

There's nothing wrong with the *Daily Mail.*

HARRIS: Is it your intention to let us hear the allegation, sir?

WESTWICH: Of course, I see from this I am alleged to have said 'I want to nibble your cock'.

SIMON: You bloody did, too.

WESTWICH: Now what I have to ask myself is this. Did I, in fact say this remark and if I did in what context could I be considered to have meant it. Was it a sexual overture of some kind, or was it culinary?

JAMIESON: Sir . . . May I say that in a structural career context *vis à vis* my future, I feel that . . .

HARRIS: Jamieson, you're in the police force, lad, not the sociology department of Leeds University.

FEAVER: My daughter's going to Leeds University.

HARRIS: Yes . . .

WESTWICH: Shut up. Now let us assume that I did say such a thing, then we are faced with a situation where a practising homosexual is in charge of a squad designed to eliminate the public disorder associated with the vice in question. This may not be entirely a bad thing.

JAMIESON: Sir . . .

WESTWICH: We must remember that certain homosexual acts are no longer illegal especially when performed in private and –

SIMON: Did you say it?

WESTWICH: Please, I was about to ask myself that question.

FEAVER: Shall I ask you, sir?

WESTWICH: No, no, no.

JAMIESON: Sir . . .

WESTWICH: Did I say these words, in other words am I, or might I be, a practising homosexual in terms of the 1967 act. The answer to that must be, as we see from the evidence here . . . yes.

JAMIESON: Sir, I wish to state that I request a transfer to CSI Feaver's office.

WESTWICH: I beg your pardon?

JAMIESON: I am requesting a transfer, sir.

WESTWICH: Why Jamieson?

JAMIESON: Because he's there, sir.

WESTWICH: Jamieson . . .

JAMIESON: If you don't mind me saying so, with you, you never know where you are. One day up, the next day down. It's confusing, sir. With the super we always had our lunch at a quarter to one and we were back at two fifteen at the latest.

WESTWICH: *Jamieson, this is a departmental meeting of the Indecency Subsection of the Vice Squad, not a kind of three dimensional lonely hearts' club.*

HARRIS: People have problems, sir.

WESTWICH: I have problems, you lot for a start.

SIMON: I'm going to get up, take that tape, walk out of that room . . .

FEAVER: Silence in court.

WESTWICH: Thank you, Feaver. Now, where was I?

FEAVER: You were a practising homosexual in the terms of the '67 act, sir.

WESTWICH: Good. Now, I must point out to PC Simon that it is not against the law to ask to nibble someone's cock.

SIMON: It bloody is.

WESTWICH: It all depends on whose cock you want to nibble.

SIMON: It's against the law to want to nibble mine.

JAMIESON: May I say, sir, that human relations and human feelings are as much a part of the complex business of running a multi-layered institution as are the ulterior aims of that institution.

WESTWICH: No you may not! Now, the question now before us is, was PC Simon a consenting adult at the time and was it his intention to get his cock nibbled. I should remind the inquiry that he was wearing ladies underwear and a bra at the time. May I also cite the transcript page two and I quote 'Come into me like a train with your proud organ'. This is not the remark of a normal member of the public going about his business.

SIMON: Look, you are a poof, that's all I'm saying.

WESTWICH: I know, I know, I know, I therefore find myself not guilty under rule.

SIMON: Bloody fix.

WESTWICH: Feaver?

FEAVER: I think you're wonderful, sir, I love you and I need your body.

SIMON: Wonderful! What's so wonderful about you?

WESTWICH: What is so wonderful, Simon, is that I am responsible for this squad and that includes you.

SIMON: Too bloody right, it does, mate.

WESTWICH: May I point out that you are here in connection with a homosexual offence of one C. Breen.

SIMON: Offence, I was set up. You're a perfect collection of benders, you're a fine bunch to talk.

WESTWICH: That being the case, and in the light of the proceedings here today, I confine the entire squad to the closet.

SIMON: The what?

WESTWICH: The closet.

JAMIESON: The closet.

HARRIS: The closet, lad, didn't they teach you anything at training college.

JAMIESON: Not the closet, I can't take the closet.

JAMIESON *dances on the table.*

WESTWICH: *Get down!* This is not music and movement.

JAMIESON: No, sir, it's tap-dancing, homosexuals are very fond of tap-dancing.

WESTWICH: I tell you, if this continues, I will confine you to the closet.

HARRIS: But it hasn't been used since the Barnes' Seascouts' annual outing.

SIMON: Where is this closet you keep going on about? I don't believe it exists, it's just a word you . . .

WESTWICH: Wrong again, Simon . . . There it is.

The doors at the back fly open to reveal the closet, a cavernous room with a bare light bulb and the odd broom against the walls etc.

JAMIESON: Here it is, the one and only, original closet.

HARRIS: How long, sir?

WESTWICH: Indefinitely.

FEAVER: Can I raise a point, sir? If we are confined to the closet, who will be undertaking indecency squad duties?

JAMIESON: 'im.

SIMON: I beg your pardon. You what?

JAMIESON: Well, you're as pure as the bleedi' driven snow, you do it.

WESTWICH: There is an interesting point, here, do people feel that public order would be better maintained by a heterosexual uncorruptible policeman, or do people rather feel that the public order would be better maintained by, and I quote 'a bunch of poofs'.

HARRIS: I think the first option is viable, sir.'

FEAVER: I agree, sir.

WESTWICH: I therefore appoint you temporary CO, ISQU.

FEAVER: PC Simon, you will proceed to the closet where you will confine the rest of the squad during which time you will endeavour to prevent all acts of gross indecency in the UK.

SIMON: Am I in charge, now, sir?

WESTWICH: You are, Simon.

SIMON: Will they go in, if I tell them, sir?

WESTWICH: They ought to.

SIMON: Right. At ease. Get in, get in, you horrible load of perverted bastards.

All of the squad apart from FEAVER and WESTWICH go into the closet.

SIMON (*to* FEAVER): And you sanctimonious old poof, get in. Don't think you aren't included you double-faced bender.

WESTWICH: Goodbye, Simon. I hope you realise the immense weight of responsibility you have got. You will have to have eyes in the back of your head. We will be in there, they will be out there. Who knows, maybe even now, as we speak, you yourself are falling prey to the appalling temptations offered to you by your chosen profession. Goodnight for now.

WESTWICH *goes into the closet and closes the door after him.*

SIMON: Get in, get in. That's the place for you lot. Maybe now normal people can get on with their life and play golf and walk their dogs without you lot trying to penetrate their bodies in disgusting ways. You stay right where you are, OK?

ALL: Young man etc.

The squad emerge from the closet singing YMCA by The Village People.

SIMON: Get back in there, I locked the door.

WESTWICH: You heard, it's not dinner time, yet.

HARRIS: Sorry, sir, the men are a bit skittish . . .

But the squad are overjoyed to be out of the closet and difficult to control.

SIMON: *Back, back.*

WESTWICH: Yes, back. Goodnight, sir, for now.

Eventually they all return to the closet and the doors are closed again.

SIMON: No one is allowed out of the closet. I'm in charge, OK? I'm out here and you're out there and let's keep it that way. Let's try and make it a place where people who believe in Sunday Lunch and Family Life and Patriotism can live without you lot trying to undermine their bodies in disgusting ways. *Nobody is allowed out of the closet.*

All of the men burst through the doors in a fine chorus line singing YMCA once more.

WESTWICH: Order. Order. Order.

SIMON: Get back.

WESTWICH: They don't seem to be in the mood, I'm afraid. Simon, it doesn't seem possible to keep them in the closet.

SIMON: Well, tell them they must stay in the closet.

WESTWICH: I'm afraid that, up to a certain point, that is their decision.

HARRIS: I think the men just want a bit of fun, sir.

They are still singing YMCA.

SIMON: It's that noise.

WESTWICH: Tell you what, they can stay out, if they sing quietly. You won't notice them.

FEAVER: *Quiet.*

WESTWICH: There, that's not too bad is it?

SIMON: Please tell me, is this really happening?

WESTWICH; God knows.

They continue to sing very quietly but suddenly burst out loudly.

SIMON: I can't think with that noise going on.

HARRIS: Hold it.

WESTWICH: What's the matter with you, Simon, what are you so worried about?

SIMON: I don't think I want to stay in the police force, sir.

WESTWICH: No? Why ever not.

SIMON: No, sir – I don't fancy it, sir.

The noise stops.

WESTWICH: So you wish to resign. I'll have your uniform.

Total silence.

SIMON: Now, sir?

WESTWICH: Now. And the underpants.

SIMON: Look . . .

WESTWICH: They're police property, Simon.

SIMON: Stop it! Stop it! Stop it!

HARRIS: Off with them! Off with them!

WESTWICH: What a magnificent one.

HARRIS: It's tremendous, sir. I haven't seen one as big as that since I was in the army.

SIMON: Stop it! Stop it! Stop it!

WESTWICH: I don't think he likes it out here.

SIMON: I don't! I hate it! I hate it!

FEAVER: We could put him in the closet, sir.

WESTWICH: You have a point, at the moment I think he's more a danger to public order than we are. Very well, you may put him in the closet, but you must promise to behave in good order and to return to the closet for curfew.

ALL: No.

HARRIS: No way, sir.

WESTWICH: What do you mean, no way?

HARRIS: Some of the men have been talking, sir. And we've had enough of the closet. We find it stifling and we're dying to stay out and sing.

WESTWICH: You'll do nothing of the kind.

HARRIS: OK?

WESTWICH: Listen!

SIMON: No!

They start to sing.

WESTWICH: Order! Order! Order!

FEAVER: You can join us if you like.

WESTWICH: What'll Divisional Headquarters, say?

JAMIESON: Divisional Headquarters can fuck themselves, sir. We've had enough of Divisional HQ.

WESTWICH: You what?

JAMIESON: We're not ordinary run-of-the-mill coppers, sir. We have special needs and special dreams. We don't want five-a-side football and six pints of lager in The Green man. We're not up for getting people to blow into little bags or knee-capping people in cells miles below ground. We're a new kind of policeman and we want to express ourselves in our own way.

WESTWICH: I knew we were working towards a more liberal police force, but this is ridiculous.

JAMIESON: Come on, sir, and assert your solidarity with us.

WESTWICH: What else will you do all day. I take it you don't intend to investigate acts of gross indecency in the UK.

JAMIESON: No, sir, we plan to commit them, not solve them.

WESTWICH: And what else will you do?

JAMIESON: Sing, sir.

WESTWICH: You are appalling, Jamieson.

JAMIESON: Sing with us, sir, say you don't give a fuck about anything really, sir. That all you want to do is raise your hands to the heavens and celebrate the mystery of life by the movements of your body and the twang, twang of your vocal cords.

WESTWICH: Oh, all right.

And, finally, COMMANDER WESTWICH *joins with them. Grand Finale plus bowing.*

Epilogue

Spoken by COMMANDER WESTWICH.

Person or persons represented
In our play – are not intended,
We promise you, to be
This commander or that PC.
Law is our subject, law our bible,
And that includes the law of libel.
Our purpose was to entertain
Anything else we here disdain,
So criticise our words or diction.
But please remember – this was fiction.
Some details I will be quite frank,
Both of procedure and of rank
Are drawn from life quite word for word,
But not the whole, it's too absurd
To contemplate a hero so not nice
Or think of such a happy end for vice.
The events you've witnessed here have been created
Not written up or heaven help us simulated.
And none of these constables existed.
I didn't want to say this, but our lawyers insisted.

SIMON *is screaming in the closet.*

FEAVER: What was that?

WESTWICH: Oh, some old closet queen.

ALL: Evening all.